T5-ARO-745

WESTERN ART

ALSO BY DEBORA GREGER

Movable Islands (1980)

And (1985)

The 1002nd Night (1990)

Off-Season at the Edge of the World (1994)

Desert Fathers, Uranium Daughters (1996)

God (2001)

WESTERN ART

DEBORA GREGER

P E N G U I N   P O E T S

PENGUIN BOOKS
Published by the Penguin Group
Penguin Group (USA) Inc., 375 Hudson Street, New York, New York 10014, U.S.A.
Penguin Group (Canada), 10 Alcorn Avenue, Toronto, Ontario, Canada M4V 3B2 (a division of
Pearson Penguin Canada Inc.)
Penguin Books Ltd, 80 Strand, London WC2R 0RL, England
Penguin Ireland, 25 St Stephen's Green, Dublin 2, Ireland (a division of Penguin Books Ltd)
Penguin Group (Australia), 250 Camberwell Road, Camberwell, Victoria 3124, Australia (a division of
Pearson Australia Group Pty Ltd)
Penguin Books India Pvt Ltd, 11 Community Centre, Panchsheel Park, New Delhi - 110 017, India
Penguin Group (NZ), cnr Airborne and Rosedale Roads, Albany, Auckland, New Zealand (a division
of Pearson New Zealand Ltd)
Penguin Books (South Africa) (Pty) Ltd, 24 Sturdee Avenue, Rosebank, Johannesburg 2196,
South Africa

Penguin Books Ltd, Registered Offices:
80 Strand, London WC2R 0RL, England

First published in Penguin Books 2004

10 9 8 7 6 5 4 3 2 1

Copyright © Debora Greger, 2004
All rights reserved

Page ix constitutes an extension of this copyright page.

LIBRARY OF CONGRESS CATALOGING IN PUBLICATION DATA
Greger, Debora——
Western art / Debora Greger.
p. cm.
ISBN 0-14-303421-9
1. Art–Poetry. I. Title.

PS3557.R42W47 2004
811'.54–dc22   2004044575

Printed in the United States of America
Set in Catull
Designed by Ginger Legato

Except in the United States of America, this book is sold subject to the condition that it shall
not, by way of trade or otherwise, be lent, resold, hired out, or otherwise circulated with-
out the publisher's prior consent in any form of binding or cover other than that in which
it is published and without a similar condition including this condition being imposed on
the subsequent purchaser.

The scanning, uploading and distribution of this book via the Internet or via any other means
without the permission of the publisher is illegal and punishable by law. Please purchase only
authorized electronic editions, and do not participate in or encourage electronic piracy of
copyrighted materials. Your support of the author's 1 rights is appreciated.

for William Logan

ACKNOWLEDGMENTS

Antioch Review: "Birds of America"

Columbia: "The Golden Horn"

Kenyon Review: "Amy in the Afterworld," "On the Oregon Trail,"
"The Palace at Four A.M.," "Venice Despoiled by Time"

Literary Imagination: "The Latin Doctors of Archer City, Texas"

MARGIE: "Musée des Beaux Arts," "On Capitol Hill"

New England Review: "Annunciation, with Missing Panel," "The Girl on
the Aqueduct," "The Male Model"

The New Republic: "Eurydice in Istanbul"

The New Yorker: "Poetry and Sleep," "A Walk in the Unconscious"

Paris Review: "The Trompe l'Oeil of History"

Parnassus: "In the Hide"

Ploughshares: "Early Man"

Poetry: "The Mosaic of Creation," "Sacra Conversazione"

Salmagundi: "Flying to Byzantium," "In the Late Holy Roman Empire,"
"Parisian Scenes," "Woman of the Tar Pits"

Sewanee Review: "Letter to a Later Roman," "Portraits: Self and Other,"
"To an Empty Case"

Southwest Review: "London Elegies," "Passiontide," "Patron Saint
of Lost Things"

Threepenny Review: "The Night Wedding"

Western Humanities Review: "The Dead and the Live Lagoon"

Yale Review: "The Alligator Bride and Groom," "In the Sixties,"
"Prince of the Powers of the Air"

–You say that art must not excite desire, said Lynch. I told you that one day I wrote my name in pencil on the backside of the Venus of Praxiteles in the Museum. Was that not desire?

–I speak of normal natures, said Stephen. You also told me that when you were a boy in that charming carmelite school you ate pieces of dried cowdung.

–James Joyce,
A Portrait of the Artist as a Young Man

CONTENTS

I

II

III

WESTERN ART

I

We spoke of the quality of the blue in the stained-glass windows of Chartres, which modern science had not been able to reproduce, as though the medieval craftsman who had produced it was a colleague. He had, we knew, billed his diocese for the purchase of sapphires ground up to create that color. Modern science had, at least, established that sapphires played no part in its composition at all. It was our first, most scholarly appreciation of the padded expense account.

—Renata Adler

I. Time Clipping the Wings of Love

Et l'homme est las d'écrire et la femme d'aimer.

—Charles Baudelaire

Wings chipped by time, a statue of Cupid
couldn't face the steps from the Tuileries
to the Louvre. I know how he felt.
O Paris, city of love, city of stairs!

A stone's long throw across the Seine
from Notre Dame, and five flights up,
the room we had: the ceiling sloped,
becoming the wall. Rising from bed,

I would forget and hit my head,
my arm—I know how the Venus de Milo felt.
Oh, to lie back down in a few centuries
of dirt, undisturbed! The hour was late,

the man tired of writing, the woman of love.
Under the skylight, under the rain,
we lay. Close enough to touch,
rain turned to silence, silence to snow.

Somewhere else it was warmer briefly:
a penguin, courting, would offer its mate
a pebble stolen from another nest.
And what about the explorer's wife, back home?

Her husband, three years from France,
named the birds and their cold coast for her.
O Terre Adélie! I think of you,
mapped like the water stain on a ceiling in Paris,

above a woman tired of writing, a man of love.
His wings clipped by time, the son
of Venus refuses to climb another flight.
O Paris, city of stairs, city of love!

II. À Mon Seul Désir

Rappelez-vous l'objet que nous vîmes, mon âme.

—Charles Baudelaire

Remember the things we saw on the edge of Paris?
The street market old, the street *nouveau arrivé*—
was it loneliness laid out its wares with love
next to seven kinds of crêpes?

Off to the side on Sunday mornings
stood a woman *d'un certain âge,*
dressed as if for church or lunch.
Her arms in the air like a whore's

indifferently displayed a dress
from the suitcase at her well-shod feet.
Clothes of a saint, or those that brushed against one—
my soul, which class of relics were hers?

Here was the lady from the last tapestry
at the Cluny, later in life, no unicorn in sight.
Where was her tent woven with tears of gold,
flying its motto as if on a battlefield?

The words the medieval weaver had tied down
with rope—were they best translated
To my sole desire, or should they be
According to my will?

She stood on her woolen island, alone.
Long lost the necklace she'd put on—
no, laid back down in its casket.
Was there a man, long gone,

for whom she'd made herself more
or less beautiful? There was
no loneliness like hers,
love come to this, to the marketplace.

III. The Painters of Days Gone By

Mais où sont les neiges d'antan?

—François Villon

Left or right, on which bank of the Seine
were the long, pale rooms of goose-fleshed women
forever bathing? Out of love or boredom,
they wouldn't meet the painter's gaze

but turned their bare backs, those wives,
those less-than-grand *horizontales*.
It was the endless summer of Impressionism,
flowers troweled on canvas in white heat.

The men who'd stood in snow to paint—
Monet, and sometimes Pissarro,
and that Englishman whose snow turned to mud—
where are they now? Blue in the shadows,

pink where the light caught a limb
and wouldn't let go until it left a bruise
of mauve: skin like a woman's
they gave to the snow.

The guard turned aside to blow on her hands.
Where was the snow of years gone by?
That long-ago winter we lived on the Charles,
you lay on a mattress on the floor,

snow no good for anything
but something animal. I lay next to you.
The ice fishermen stood on the river,
waiting for want to make something come closer.

7

THE PALACE AT FOUR A.M.

Who's sleeping next to you?
It's not loneliness–it's your wife.

–Nazim Hikmet

And then one morning the courtship is over.
No longer does the male hold forth at four A.M.

to impress the female enough to mate.
Now only the note of alarm is given voice

by the blackbird or its cheeky, petrified young:
a *chink* in the air–as if stone were being dressed,

the way you mend a wall in an old cathedral town,
the local clunch too soft to last. Almost fifty,

you wake almost alone, in a foreign country.
That's not a husband next to you, it's loneliness.

You can hear the electric whine of the milk float,
muezzin of the neighborhood, a few doors down,

near the mosque once Methodist chapel–
but who worships it now? The *chink* of bottle against stone

drowns under the dead weight of casks being rolled
down to the cellar of the Live and Let Live pub.

The wind is wrong, but the hour's quartered
and tolled by Our Lady of the English Martyrs.

O Fisher, Campion, and More, admit to your circle
Hikmet, Communist, poet exiled to Russia and there

kept company by a woman younger and blonder
than his wife. For this small warmth let us give thanks.

I. Rembrandt by Himself

There were more Rembrandts by Rembrandt
than ever before, down in the basement

of the museum. How he liked to dress up:
a helmet like a chamber pot, with matching gorget.

A plume with a mind of its own. Upholstered in velvet,
chained in gold, he painted himself into the past—

but couldn't get the feet right, as the x-ray showed,
and put in a poodle, desperation kinking every curl.

He'd never work full-length again, but forgot
he was right-handed, faithful only to the mirror

constant in its lies. You saw him age before your—
no, his—very eyes, until he was old at thirty-six

though not yet bankrupt. His wife had died—
no, he'd keep her alive, make himself not yet born,

the world extending no farther than the window
he would draw himself looking from, his turban

vaguely Turkish: just a man seeking an odd star
to the east, over the IJsselmeer.

Men on one side, women on the other:
portrait miniatures faced one another

as if for an evening of dancing before a little war—
the way we'd been arranged in grade school.

In the last row, dime-size, gold-encased, hung two
that were all eye: the eye of the beloved,

whoever she once was. Was the guard's back turned?
You had to be eye to eye to see that the iris

was just another earth. Aqueous humor blue,
green continents adrift: the world was tiny

two hundred years ago, all love inconsequent.
O my pretty unknown, to whose watch chain

were you fobbed? To what did you turn a blind blue eye?
A slaver eased from its slip, bound for the Gold Coast—

were you aboard? Your painter would have required,
in greatest haste, more ivory blanks, the finest grade.

III. Gainsborough by Himself

Was he bored? Deep in Suffolk,
Gainsborough had already warned one lord

it wouldn't pay to encourage him out of his way;
better to buy an Old Master. For there

it was two days' ride to the nearest lemon.
Were he back in Bath, he'd have ordered

the little oak table brought to the parlor,
laid with sand and moss, and knobs of coal

made to sit for rocks against a distant woods
of broccoli. Forget the lake, a broken mirror.

After a certain age, who can bear to look out the window?
Time on his hands like paint, he painted himself

in the muddy colors he loved most of all.
His face won't bear the weight of his looking

for much longer, but he doesn't know that yet.
Death, his last patron, will say of it,

Can't you see? There's something wrong with the eyes.

Holding the dead bird by the feet,
he seemed to offer it—to me, right there in the museum.

Did they eat bittern in the seventeenth century?
The bird has almost vanished from those parts,

but the foreground was filled with feathers,
the wings, rarely used, fallen open in death.

The man behind this drab, failed camouflage
was a young Rembrandt, sporting his first mustache.

He gave nothing away but the bird he'd bagged,
keeping us—no, himself—in the varnished Dutch dark.

There I stood, reflected in the latest layer
of lacquer: younger, at a ditch in Florida,

trying not to breathe, not wanting to disturb
a speckled wading bird I'd need help to name:

least bittern, immature, the field guide claimed.
There is no bitterness like his. Call it love,

the fine vermiculation on wing and back,
so difficult, it was said, *to admire on the living.*

In a cozy cottage
at the end of the road, two old Communists
     made us tea,

then showed us the way. Their house too hot,
     the Cold War cooled—
you must live, Marx said, to enter history.

          But what did he know?
To enter the hide, you must keep quiet,
     the sign said

at the blind on the fens. Binoculars bristled
     at our invasion.
Telescopes stood their ground. I looked out

          the window slits.
The pond ready to surrender to ice,
     the sun to give up,

but still, from Iceland, from Siberia,
     more swans swam
over East Anglia. They called in the cold

          for their mates,
the lake littered with big white birds—
     a ream of paper

crumpled. As if property were still theft.
     As if young Shelley
still tore the endpapers from borrowed books,

good socialist,
and folded the pages into boats.
What did he know

about mating for life? A swan could,
out of grief,
drag a sheep to water and hold it under.

AMY IN THE AFTERWORLD

in memory of Amy Clampitt

A blue flame coursed across the willow
　　　where it wept into the river,
　　　　　keeping low–
　　　a jewel lost from its setting,
　　　　　a ring sinking–
and then I realized I'd seen a kingfisher.

I knew it from the cover of your book.
　　　You were five years gone,
　　　　　the river Cam still,
　　　as always, sluggish enough
　　　　　for slime and lily.
A single fisherman, out early, caught nothing.

The police had dragged it for something,
　　　if only to give the frogmen
　　　　　some exercise:
　　　bicycles and a fax machine
　　　　　roped in river weed
lay where they'd been thrown to the bank.

As if they'd been hauled from under the river,
　　　having failed to deliver a message
　　　　　to the underworld.
　　　In death you wander green fields,
　　　　　the Egyptians thought,
longing for a better crop than they'd ever seen.

Longing for Iowa, that state of being you left,
    as soon as you could, for the city—
        or was it the open water?
    I wanted to tell you how the chemist,
        as ancient as his shop,
sensed something foreign in the way I asked

for Band-Aids, not "plasters." Once he'd been
    as far as the Holy Land,
        he told me,
    where he'd found himself
        in the desert
surrounded by a gang of Arab boys

who had among them just enough English
    to make clear their demand.
        Where was he from?
        "*England,*" one of them repeated.
        "London. Rain."
As if that were paradise enough. But I was too late.

I. History of the World

He told me merrily that it was to be called the "Painter's Wife's Island,"
saying that whilst the fellow drew that map, his wife sitting by,
desired him to put in one country for her, that she,
in imagination, might have an island of her own.

—Sir Walter Ralegh, *History of the World*

There by the river squatted the Tower of London,
guarded by ravens glossy as ministers,

fed on raw beef. They wagged their feathered beards.
What sentence was there left to pronounce

but mated for life? The good husband
Ralegh's rooms were empty, he the ghost

who strolled the river wall to be seen
for what he was: gardener the queen called "Water,"

mocking his country accent to show her favor,
while it lasted. Why should he finish writing

the history of the world? Death waited
in a warm climate, but not for a minor poet of love,

king of the Indies, self-proclaimed—
no, for the son he sent up the Orinoco to his death.

How did we miss the Crown Jewels, love?
Looking for gold, we found the instruments

of persuasion, so prettily named.
Catherine's Wheel. The Scavenger's Daughter,

designed to force the blood through the skin
to make its own confession.

II. A Game of Chess

What you get married for if you don't want children?

—T. S. Eliot, *The Waste Land*

Twenty years unmarried, the anniversary dinner over,
but, like the long-wedded, we sat in silence.

The singer, long-winded, sang Sinatra
in Italian to the all-but-empty restaurant

and then that Orpheus on the Thames
pulled up a chair to smoke and watch.

Where were the women to tear him apart?
I was the only female in the room

except for two queens on a chessboard, hiding
behind the pawns, waiting to flash their skirts.

It was your move, love. Did you play the game of kings
or just spend money like an American?

A Roman and an Englishman wanted to know.
It was the chef's move, coached by the waiter,

who played in *two* leagues, London and county.
I gave up my seat across from you and wandered,

lonely as the cloud of suds that crowned a king
of dirty dishes tilted in the kitchen sink,

waiting to be toppled by some opposing queen.
This happened somewhere near the Serpentine,

that dead queen's manmade lake
with a bend like the birth canal.

I speak of the mother of George III.
In the washroom mirror, someone all in black,

regnant, looked at me, unchecked.
It was my move. It meant nothing to me.

III. The Remains of the Rose

Man: *And who hath layne with you to night?*
Wife: *I haue been with Nobody.*
—*Nobody and Somebody*

And then, without warning, an armada of winds
from the Bay of Biscay conquered England,

for a day. That was summer, all discontent.
On the south bank of the Thames,

American dollars hammered a new Globe
into a rudely theatrical O.

To reach the past you had to cross the street
to the hole just dug with dental picks

and then swept clean with a toothbrush: the ruins
of the Rose. Like a jawbone the outer wall curved,

exposed—a theater of memory.
Who stood under the work light on the dirt stage?

A woman played by a boy? No, there I was,
somebody in an old farce now out of fashion;

but still it played, at least to foreigners,
as Shakespeare's men had found in Germany.

Nobody and Somebody, the true historie—
Love, put on the endlessly sad trousers,

the traditional costume. I, in a shirt as big
as a bedsheet, need my other half to give me grief.

IV. A Night at the Byron Hotel

*Rakitin: As if you didn't know what it is to be in the presence of
someone you love and yet who bores you stiff.*

*Natalya Petrovna: "Love," that's a powerful word. You're being
a bit too clever for me.*

—Ivan Turgenev, *A Month in the Country*

Something Byronic, something Levantine—
the rooms were named for faraway places.

It was lost on me, but not on the Pakistani porter,
who handed you the key to a closet—no, a postage stamp.

A television had been bolted to the ceiling.
There was no getting around the bed,

which would have to be swum like the Hellespont,
whether to the door or to you.

The late-night forecaster beamed down on us,
promising, as always on that British isle,

"Rain, followed by showers." Looking for better weather,
you flicked the channels. Where was a western

when you needed it? A white man in a white hat
saving cattle for democracy—O sun and dust!

We'd been to the theater earlier, a play
where gentlefolk with a house in the country

went there to be miserable. It was famous.
You'd fallen asleep in the second act,

just as the aging actress fell upon the tutor;
and I'd kept watch. Had we ever been closer?

V. The Whispering Gallery

And now good-morrow to our waking soules,
Which watch not one another out of feare.

–John Donne, *The Good-Morrow*

What could I say? You were away
on the other side of the cathedral,

waiting for me to whisper in your ear
from where I stood. Far below,

deep in St. Paul's, the others trailed,
ants trooping their colors raggedly,

tomb to tomb. Donne's was the only one
to survive the Great Fire, the guidebook claimed,

but what did the dead dean care?
Who disrobed for him now, mistress or priest?

Before, behind, between, above, below,
the ants had roved his bones

and then moved on to some newfound land,
like Ralegh's men to Roanoke.

O my American! My back to the drop,
I wanted only to hug the ground,

not you, but first I would have to move.
All I could think of, I said to the wall.

And then had to say it over, louder,
so that a stranger, edging past,

moved faster, begging my pardon:
"I love you." It came close enough to truth.

II

What can be sadder than to sink and never be able to rise again by any act of the will? From being a Frenchman, one falls to the level of a cosmopolitan, of just anyman, and from there to the level of a mollusk.

–Jules Michelet

THE MOSAIC OF CREATION

I. The First Day: The Separation of Light from Darkness

High in the dark light we call weak,
God has six days. He's young, smooth-cheeked—

and already something's not to his taste,
an angel, as always, in too-great haste

to roll the earth back into night
before he can say, "Wait. There should be light."

In the dull gold light come raining down
the distance turning it to brown,

the angel looks about to cry—
but that comes later, if God stays dry.

Water has risen at his back
but he's Venetian—he only cracks

where the building does, across his arm—
oh, to keep him from further harm!

The very first day—what should he do?
The face of the waters gives no clue.

Look, from the basilica's great porch—
the water flickers from torch to torch.

II. The Third Day: The Separation of the Seas and Dry Land

And on the third day God is stuck
with too much water, just his luck—

where's he to stand in this blue mess
to call forth all he's yet to bless,

the little things he'll be known for,
a burning bush, a wise man's star?

Does the young God heave an almighty sigh?
He's left the water out to dry

and stepped to a green that doesn't give way.
For, look, an angel seems to say,

now he'll have to figure out
what to do with it—perhaps a sprout

or two, a fish with feet or wings.
Far below, a choir of humans sings

for practice: once again a phrase
slops at his ankles like a wave.

This is Venice, the edge of the world
he parted the waters from, the swirled

blue tiles the one thing he doesn't bless.
The water does what it does best,

without his help, taking the land
back from under his outstretched hand.

III. Adam and Eve in Hiding

It slides, the voice of the soprano,
up the scale, trying to tiptoe, to stay *piano*.

It snakes up the cupola into the garden
where Adam and Eve would like to stay hidden:

God, out for his daily walk,
would like to have a moment's talk

about the fruit at their disposal
and whether they *do* know good from evil

since there's a fig leaf in Adam's hand
to cover himself, though there's no wind.

Not a breath of cold yet, not a leaf stirred
except by Eve to cover her words,

the air around them rich with gilt
as if something more than light has spilt

into the garden this afternoon
so endless the next scene comes too soon:

a door will open in the gold,
a door to a world where they'll grow old.

Already the leaves are tinged with fall.
How young they look, denying it all.

The bishop of St. Mark's rose from his throne.
Mantis religiosa, he bent his carapace
to celebrate High Mass.

Mandibles moved in prayer,
but something winged eluded his grasp.
Still, a man lifted a video camera

over his head like a baby to be blessed,
over the blessed and the tourist alike,
over the sign that said, over and over,

speaking in the tongues of tourists,
that photography was strictly forbidden.
Something had risen and was not there.

On Easter Sunday, a praying mantis rose
in Venice, in the natural history museum.
Larger than life, larger than us,

and motorized, from the huge leaf
where it lay in wait, it reared up.
In a room full of insects nailed to their names,

the front legs folded like hands in front of its face.
Even bread made body—enraptured,
the mantis prayed for something to devour.

Even the church we stepped into,
out of the rain, seemed already sunk.
We walked like saints walking on water,

the paved floor worn down into waves
by the ebb and flow of the saved.
What had they approached on their knees

that we couldn't see in the muddy depths?
A skirt fishtailed around a pillar—
something swam through the gloom:

a gray priest dipped a rag
in gray water and wet the stone
as if to save the dust in all its gray glory,

to save the soul, as gray as the rag wrung out,
a patch of gray light
next to a saint's shriveled thumb.

By the side altar someone had left a small suitcase
next to a bigger loaf, a wheel of bread.
The door to the empty tabernacle stood open.

He descended into hell—
seeing us dripping on his marble,
the priest disappeared into the murk, flicked a switch,

and from on high a gray chorus flooded the church.
All thy waves and thy billows are gone over me.
In the rain I had stood and watched a confectioner

in the back of his shop lick his finger
and seal a chocolate egg's dark tomb.
In the rain the stones of Venice showed their veins.

And, from midday, darkness covered the shops
of Venice, from the back-canal funeral parlor
to the one that sold miracle cures for rising damp.

At death's door, the black gondola was moored,
ready to row the body to the isle of the dead.
Lilies had been laid out in long boxes.

Linens shrouded sandwiches left unbought.
Like a dead man, forgotten, like a thing thrown away–
even the church was locked, the one where we'd seen

how the crucifix had been lowered from the wall
and laid to rest, propped on a pillow
on the deathly pale floor.

Skinned, pink as the reborn,
the paschal lamb hung by its hooves
in the butcher's darkened window.

How much would thirty pieces of silver bring?
Even the money changers outside the church
were closed. Even American Express.

Oh, not to be standing around,
trying to look holy rather than vacant,
as the Virgin took forever to show off her baby!

The saints on the wall scarcely looked up,
they were so rapt, alone with the Alone at last.
Seeing one baby, you've seen them all?

His nose in a lofty but lightweight book,
Aquinas had nothing to say on the subject,
though conversation in heaven, he'd read,

like kissing over great distance,
left the lips supremely satisfied.
Alone with the Alone, should not a doctor

who found himself there talk to a virgin martyr?
I saw a Saint Ursula in leather jacket,
looking as if she'd just awakened.

Where was the daydream a painter had given her
long ago? There, beside the bed, an angel appeared,
unasked, robes gray, wings colorless.

Guessing her size, Death held out a shroud.

THE NIGHT WEDDING

in una maniera paolesca

Just bystanders from the wrong century
who'd stepped from the Accademia
and turned a corner into a Veronese in the rain—
still, we waited outside the English church.

Pigeon inquisitors puffed their gray chests.
Why had the artist included foreigners
in such a sacred scene? they wanted to know.
It was July, 1573.

A door of light pierced the side of the dark
and from it red velvet bled:
four *cinquecento* trumpeters in dampened doublets
raised their horns, but no sound came

except the little whips of rain.

after Tiepolo

I. The Meeting of Antony and Cleopatra

Because the painter knew that history,
when it happened, happened in Venice,
it's on the steps of the Riva

that Cleopatra meets Antony's ship.
And it's not so long ago, merely the Renaissance,
so high it smells like the Grand Canal,

which lies hidden in the fresco
behind her froth-white, useless horse,
his unseaworthy, shell-like ship.

In its ghostly ballroom, you stand,
feeling underdressed, and study the painted ceiling,
the peeling walls, waiting to have seen something . . .

a rustle of silk vanished in a forest of spears?

II. The Feast of Cleopatra

The past is in the *next* room,
the painter would have us believe,
and the food's better—

a dog still waits at the feet of its mistress,
like love for table scraps.
But Cleopatra has called only for a glass

of vinegar, she's so extravagant.
Holding a pearl earring,
she reaches for the goblet,

ready to prove to Antony,
girded in armor for this battle across the table—
whatever it was she proved.

But not quite yet.
Pliny still wants to know of the pearl,
do we get the most bodily pleasure

from the luxuries that cost a life?
Where before they only dove for pearls,
now the poor divers desire them, he says.

See how a jewel attends a lady like a slave.
How a pearl warms to the skin.
This he calls natural history

for want of a better word. But not yet.
Not yet does love begin at the beginning,
acidly, its slow dissolve.

THE DEAD AND THE LIVE LAGOON

How doth the city sit solitary, that was full of people!
How she is become as a widow! She that was great
among the provinces, how she is become tributary!

—Lamentations 1:1

I. Barrier Island

Venice lay in the water, it lay in the dark.
The morning after Carnival, only a pigeon,
one foot clubbed, hobbled along,
hoping for a crumb outside of Florian's.

Day-old confetti would have to do.
This was the hour a club-footed ghost might slip
into the Grand Canal before it could wake
a last vaporetto of lost souls.

Death stroked its way to the Lido
as if a ghost horse were still stabled there,
waiting to be ridden down the silt—
down the salt, past the later casino,

the horse of the English lord who wrote,
If I am shovelled into the Lido Churchyard—
in your time, let me have "implora pace"
and nothing else for my epitaph.

Death was unmoved, and you—you fell asleep
in Byron's old house, under the nose of the guard.
Under the noses of all the dead doges
whose dark portraits were hung on high

in a palazzo now the Costume Institute.
Where once his mistress and his monkey
had screamed and torn his hair,
a mannequin posed in a riding coat like his,

embroidered with brags, and turned a pocked face,
plastered, toward us: of what earthly use
were we in that once grand apartment,
so painstakingly, so pointlessly restored?

Something was burning—you could smell it
even before we reached the island
to which the glass furnaces had been banished.
Better that Murano burn than Venice,

the doges had decided, and death to any master
of the mirror who sold the secret abroad.
In the glass museum, an alembic stood, beheaded,
as an old retort bent low its long neck for the ax—

but the great age of the mirror was over,
and of the chandelier, and the little age
of the ornamental ashtray was drawing to a close.
Who needed a reliquary, a hand-blown ampule?

In the Byzantine church, I had to view the Virgin
through binoculars, she stood so far away.
Her hands, as long as fishing boats,
were lifted up as if to push us back—

to the souvenir shops that lined the canal,
and the recycling bins at their doors,
as if whatever glass gauds we bought
were best sacrificed to the gods on the spot.

In a mirror gone dark with age,
who was the ghost woman whose gaze I caught?
Here, where the past was melted down and resold,
how could it be myself-to-come that I saw?

III. Island of Saint and Sea Dragon

I believe in the cold, I thought.
Through the merely man-size door
cut in a god-size one, we entered
the church of San Giorgio Maggiore

and felt the drop in temperature.
I believed in the cold, the weather almighty,
the radiator too small to heat heaven and earth.
The large, dark paintings were all about food:

on some mainland, a spinning wheel stood still,
a fire laid. Washerwomen slapped a shirt.
Someone kept reading, not turning a page,
while manna was gathered in deeper shade.

Or, in Tintoretto's last *Last Supper,*
at the end of an endless table, past the peaches
untransubstantiated, two apostles still waited
to be served. A cat pawed through a basket—

I paused for breath, as when you step
from a car at the top of a mountain pass
and draw into your body a sudden chill,
defining more than the outline of the lungs.

Some soul of being, pierced—*Forgive me,*
Chekhov wrote, *if I speak of food and the cold,*
for they are my only two subjects. He had been
to Venice once, before he was Chekhov.

A young man with a slight cough, sent south
for the winter, wrote his brother, *I float through the streets.*
And in the evening! Oh Lord, my God!
In the evening, you could die. Warmth, stillness, stars . . .

IV. Island of the Redeemer

Death would come by water, I thought.
I turned my back to Venice
to count the souls in Il Redentore
on a Saturday morning—a handful

or two stood, lost, in that huge Palladian pile,
their parish church. In their winter coats—
was it colder within that extravagance of emptiness,
as minutely measured as music, or without?

Paintings were boarded up like shops,
shuttered from my unfaithful gaze—
or had they been removed? Built to thank someone
for sparing Venice from the plague,

the church tried not to echo the arch,
the ache of breath drawn. Dull as prayer learned by heart,
the grizzled light of grace spilled, missing the living.
From death, as from his hotel across the canal,

Ruskin kept his eyes closed. The only thing uglier
than a church by Palladio, he was sure,
was his wife on their wedding night. Why wasn't she
as smooth as the marble statues he adored?

Wife his *sweet forest,* his *wrecker on a rocky coast,*
his *fair mirage in the desert to be followed*
until you come to some dark salt lake of tears—
I heard the motor of a boat cough to life.

There was a note in pencil for Ezra Pound.
Pink ballet slippers in a plastic bag
hung in mid-air from Diaghilev's grave.
Brodsky didn't have a headstone yet,

just a few pebbles, balanced,
out of respect, on a wooden cross.
A cigarette and a whiskey bottle lay on the dirt,
songbirds in the cypress making light of it.

This was the island of the dead,
one stop from Venice by water-bus. This was why
the shops on the Fondamenta sold just flowers
and gravestones waiting to be given a name.

At the museum of archaeology, a boy-pharaoh lay.
Gold his limbs, lapis lazuli the head,
turquoise the hands that carried sand.
Beside him, his heart was stored in a jar.

Grant him a sailing downstream as a living soul,
a sailing upstream as a bennu bird.
He rushed at the sky as a heron. He settled
as a beetle on an empty seat of the vaporetto.

VI. Island of the Last Judgment

I loved the devil. At the back of the basilica
of the lagoon, in mosaic, he was blue.
From the churchyard came the cries
of French schoolgirls pretending to be statues.

They teetered on the ancient tombs.
Trying to stay still, they broke into shrieks,
for what good was art without an audience?
And so they wearied of their little deaths,

but not even the salt-flat taste of eternity
could force them into church. O Torcello!
No, I loved the other devil most,
the purplish one with the sidelong glance

and the hot red tip of a tongue.
They were the only ones having any fun.
True, corn poppies bloomed in paradise,
but only to be trampled by the lately saved.

The rest of the saints looked carefully
at nothing, the view from the back row
blocked by the haloes in front, arrayed
like Sunday-best plates in a china cabinet.

Lion, leopard, griffin, and a version—no, vision—
of an elephant offered the humans
they had in their mouths to the angels.
And God was grim and worked in gold.

III

You cannot conceive of anything so beautiful as Constantinople, viewed from the Golden Horn on the Bosphorus. . . . I thought Dan had got the state room pretty full of rubbish at last, but a while ago his dragoman arrived with a bran new, ghastly tombstone of the Oriental pattern, with his name handsomely carved and gilded on it in Turkish characters. That fellow will buy a Circassian slave, next.

−Mark Twain

VENICE DESPOILED BY TIME

San Marco

Still merchant seaman, still whore!
There comes a point where you make us pay
to go any further, even in church.
So much to lift the skirt, so much to see

the Byzantine booty behind the high altar.
Trapped in filigree, saints from the east
eye the son of God as he enters the city.
Toward the temple, not shown,

and the money-changers, the sellers of sacrificial doves,
an ass picks its way through precious stones,
lest the stones cry out. St. John smiles down
on emeralds embedded at the foot of the cross.

Past ruby, topaz, sapphire chased in gold—
in Constantinople, not one stone left upon another
after three days' looting by the Crusaders,
once the flames had died.

They brought horses and mules into Santa Sofia,
the better to carry off the holy vessels.
When some of those fleeing slipped and fell,
they were run through with swords—

that the Army of God might pay you for the ships.
And so there came to you the arm of the martyr Stephen,
some of the flesh of St. Paul, the Baptist's tooth,
an ampule of the Savior's blood.

You make us pay even more
to see what wasn't melted down for Bonaparte,
who preached that an army advanced on its stomach,
when he meant gold. An incense boat,

worked from dull stone to fit in the hand,
has foundered on a shelf next to the silver-gilt relief
hiding a sliver of the True Cross and one Holy Nail
from my unbelieving eye. Lord, I am unworthy.

Speak but the word now there's nothing left to burn.

Venice sinking in reflection behind us,
      now over the water
the train holds sway, the carriage swimming,
      cool with the colors
of water, students schooling like fish—

until Padua. There, into the mist they drift,
      into a fresco.
The colors still cold five centuries later,
      the drawing stiff,
some saint preaching to the rising damp,

which hangs on every word—was I among them,
      young again and sure
that art history was wasted on me?
      The campus cherry trees
had bloomed with tear gas that spring.

We pass the village Eccolino had to destroy
      in order to take.
Orchards lay themselves open to bees.
      In regimental rows,
grapevines train to bear the pruner's knife.

Anthony of Padua, preacher to princes
      who ceased and desisted,
for a while at least—preacher to the fishes,
      who were so moved
they left the water, don't let me interrupt.

Patron saint of all things lost,
      only your tongue
remains incorrupt. Let it not pray for me,
      who would not be found.
Let it wag. Let it flail in the shallows.

IN THE LATE HOLY ROMAN EMPIRE

at the tomb of Galla Placidia,
in memory of Sister Josephine, S.N.J.M.

Sister, I laid my cheek against a column
of air in the caverns of memory,
just as St. Augustine had claimed,
back in the days when I still had a soul.
Here in a little Byzantine building

where it was always cold, the emperor's mother
wasn't in her tomb, the *Blue Guide* noted.
So who had sat in death on a cypress throne?
Whose bones had been burned by those boys
who played with candles four centuries ago?

Mosaics arched over the emptiness,
over the tourists who came, shivered, and went,
fading like frescoes, their guide not finished.
A mosaic of flames roared under a grill
in one lunette, not hot enough yet

for St. Lawrence to lay himself down,
though his robe fluttered stonily closer.
"I'm done on this side. Turn me over,"
the page in the guidebook said so dryly
that across half the earth I heard you, Sister.

You read to us after lunch years ago,
in the days when I had a soul and a guardian angel.
Both found me wanting, for I had not faith
like yours, fervent, ironic, Augustinian.
I stood where you'd said we should,

in desert out west, where we had no history yet.
In Ravenna I stood in the place you'd marked
in the history book. Two deer in the last lunette
picked their way to water in a place you'd never been,
who'd entered the convent so young.

Was I to believe the deer were just two souls?
No, the artist knew his animals too well,
though the stag was made to part the leaves
for the doe with a merely human love.
Sister, is it as cold where you are?

That is no country for women. In the streets
of Istanbul men strutted like pigeons.
Like saints surrounded by gold in the old mosaics,
they wanted to sell me something.

Boys swarmed the Blue Mosque like bees, touting rugs
in what they guessed was my language.
At the bus stop on the Bosphorus, the day's fish
had been laid out to shine like souvenirs.

I wanted the big flatfish with the wandering eye.
He had the face of an angel over a tomb,
monument to his own magnificence.
In the church of St. Savior, the sainted men

painted on the wall looked down on me.
What could I do but walk beneath their gaze,
I who'd paid to look, not to pray? Over their heads,
a girl was given away to priests in the Temple.

Even higher up, an angel brought her bread,
since she would be needed later in the story,
being the young virgin Mary.
A paltry thing, a tattered coat upon a stick—

a girl at a traffic light at midnight
took the smirched rag she was supposed to smear
our windshield with, and wound it instead
around a fence post in play. Into a doll

whose face could barely be seen for the veils.
Soul, though I no longer believe in you,
we were younger once. Don't
turn away when I would talk to you.

I. The Ruined Palace

Not that long ago, said the Turkish woman,
a man took your money, filled a bucket with water,

and threw it at the mosaics. Flushed out of hiding
was all that remained of the great palace of Byzantium.

But now each tile's scrubbed as a tourist,
so a donkey seems to gawk at us as we eye his inlaid food.

This must have been the dining room; on the floor
the animals feed on one another, or flee the hunter.

Granting three days of looting as was the custom,
the young sultan had toured the palatial ruin,

sacked first by Crusaders two centuries earlier,
and been moved to quote poetry not his own:

The spider is the curtain-holder in the palace of the Caesars.
The owl hoots its night call on the towers of Aphrasaib.

Her new pink sneakers, bought from a man
with a suitcase of shoes from behind the old Iron Curtain,

who sold his wares at the illegal street market,
had heels that lit up when she walked—

but, for a six-year-old, that wasn't enough.
She tried on a golden belt in the Covered Bazaar.

Her jeans were too big, her logic Aristotelian:
it fit. She needed one—you couldn't argue,

except that this occurred at the gold merchant's,
a hole in the wall in the jewelers' precinct,

unlocked for her mother. A belt worth $24,000.
No? Perhaps a small collection of high-school rings,

the finest American? The Cold War over,
the Air Force gone home, they sat in the dust. Yes?

A woman needed an amulet to protect against the *djinns,*
lower than angels, who took the shape of men.

III. Turkish Carpet

The Virgin appeared in the least-expected places.
In the kitchens of the old imperial mosque,

now the museum of carpets, in Istanbul,
she was sighted: mother with infant asquirm,

enthroned on a gold and unforgiving chair,
red carpet rolled out—for someone had matched rugs

to Renaissance paintings (in poor reproduction).
Carpaccio, Piero, Van Eyck—they worshiped,

at her feet, each knot that had been tied
by some nomad girl, knowing no better.

Happy the long hours of child labor,
for how much longer till such an artisan

died in childbirth, her name buried beside her?
Somewhere under the Virgin's velvet hem

was the archway into which the infidel bent
his soul five times a day, mouth giving open

to the woolly next world, empty by design
save for the sketchiest of lamps.

Latest conqueror of the Ottoman empire,
I with the emerald-green dollar

to which the Turkish lira prostrated itself further—
I have seen three footprints in stone

of the prophet Mohammed, no two of which match.
A few stray beard hairs and some of his dust

housed in jeweled reliquaries. Did I believe
the tray of emeralds tossed like salad,

never to be served, in the Topkapi?
No, the bloodstained gown with mile-long sleeves

of the sultan killed by his own guards.
Where, once, severed heads had been displayed,

the marble niches of the Imperial Gate were empty
but for a pigeon bowing and scraping for my crumbs.

I brought nothing back to life, not even a woman
from the harem who'd been stitched into a sack with stones

and rowed to the Sea of Marmara. Only the taxi driver
came back the wrong way through the Gate of the Dead.

The Turkish girl on the Roman aqueduct
gestured to me to scale the wall—
or so I gathered. I lacked her language.

I lacked her fearless way with heights.
Like a washed-up Crusader, I was reduced
to taking the small hand she offered,

hauling me up to flop in the dust
of ancient slaughter, slain by my own laughter.
She was the Other. She was myself,

lost queen of the back yard and the front,
empress of the neighborhood, who led
with a fist of snow, a fist of mud.

Below, Istanbul traffic bleated, herded
through ancient arches into narrow lanes.
There stood a ram with a harem of two ewes,

on new sidewalk, waiting for the bus.
Too dirty, even, for a woman to touch,
the sky was held up by minarets.

I wanted down. And there she was again,
showing me how to fall to earth.
Fall like those golden beings, all wing,

inside the dome of the Hagia Sophia—
my knees gave way where stone would not,
though I was caught up in her small fierce hug.

Kissed on both cheeks, I walked away.
I know nothing about her but this. These words
are for her, words that make nothing happen.

EURYDICE IN ISTANBUL

What was there to complain of,
but that she had been loved?

—Ovid

I

In the city that had died twice
and been condemned to life once more,

the best rooms were booked. Garbo, Mata Hari,
the one-legged Sarah Bernhardt, Atatürk—

the dead were back at the Pera Palas.
There, up under the roof, I lay.

All over town the muezzins competed for my soul.
The tap dripped in the sink, the foul waters

of forgetfulness urging me to drink.
Love, lie down with me. Charm this old rock.

II

Under a men's club you found the underworld.
The man in the sharp suit who kept the door

led the way in the dark. He turned on a light.
The dark swallowed it. Down the stairs,

down to the cavernous Byzantine cistern,
he seemed to float. Was I to follow?

On a shaky step, I hugged the wall.
Taking the puddles in his fine shoes,

he led you on where I held back.
How could he not be shade or god?

Your whistling drifted in and out of tune,
the pillars ready to follow you back to the world,

so many trees, so many stones.
Your shadow stretched the length of a column.

It lay in the mud as if to await the boatman,
the one the old guidebooks mention—

and then, there you were again, face half aglow,
half lost. My heart emptied a chamber

by flooding another. *Let go,* it said,
through my hand, to the wall. *Let go.*

IV

In my first interview with a Sierra bear, we were frightened and embarrassed, both of us, but the bear's behavior was better than mine.

–John Muir

Remember, love,
when it was just the two of us
        and a woolly mammoth
off Wilshire Boulevard in Los Angeles?

At La Brea, its yard,
or more, of tusks embraced the air
        like ballerinas' arms,
for want of something small to gore.

It trumpeted on cue,
small motor whining at its heart.
        Like a shag rug
taking a beating, it shook itself still

before rows and rows—
one whole wall—of dire-wolf skulls.
        And one human skeleton.
In a glass coffin, a Stone Age Snow White

had gone to bone.
She was about my age when I met you
        a quarter-century ago.
I had no children. Had she borne any?

Experts still argued.
A woman her age scrubbed a jawbone
        with a toothbrush gone black,
until at last it was recognizable:

a boat to ferry
the last few teeth of a saber-tooth cat
into this afterlife.
Remember, love, that warm fall?

Tar oozed outside
into glossy pools behind high fences.
Like the carnivores
who went before us, we followed the trail;

but all we found
were a leaf, a twig, a dandelion seed, trapped.
And, unmarked on the map,
a brave new tar pit young enough to mother.

POETRY AND SLEEP

And up I rose refresh'd, and glad, and gay,
Resolving to begin that very day
These lines; and howsoever they be done,
I leave them as a father does his son.

—John Keats, *Sleep and Poetry*

What did Keats know about sleep or poetry?
He'd never seen an elephant
take a nap. Merely lying down
took the elaborate effort of a poet:

you almost saw the thought occur
behind the *massif* of forehead and then
set out to reach the extremities by dark.
Down on his back knees, the animal lowered,

a devout who baptized himself
with a trunkful of dust and straw.
He bent the front knees next,
and then the great ship of faith began to rock

until he capsized on his side,
sleep still slow to board. The small sail
of an enormous ear flapped at a fly.
The tail flicked like a rope left loose on deck.

After the dust bath, before the long drink
in the parking lot of a shopping mall,
I watched a circus elephant breathe,
the afternoon perfumed by hay and dung.

I thought of my father, in his recliner
at the angle of repose, book still open
on his chest, pages riffled by his breath,
sleep the first savannah where my mother

couldn't reach him, but not the last.

PRINCE OF THE POWERS OF THE AIR

O alienate from God, O spirit accurst,
Forsaken of all good; I see thy fall.

—John Milton, *Paradise Lost*

In Florida, where these things can happen,
I was driving south in the dead of winter—
that is to say, a day scoured of cloud.
Only sycamores were brown and sullen
against a sky from a fresco centuries old.
In the blue gone chalky but still luciferous,
a dark scream of wings arced like stone.
Black feathers fell to the grassy median.
A vulture, feeding on the center line,
hit by a car . . . I had spun over my life

like that once, when I was six.
The classroom had grown too close, the lesson long,
recess rewarded only after purgatory.
I laid my head on the desk and closed my eyes,
only to feel myself whirled into the Void,
though I didn't know the word.
I was the null to keep it company.
Who would bear me up if I fell? Oh, fall
from that high state of loneliness! Far below,
a tiny nun was busy, improving on a Bible story—

and now here you were, dark angel,
just the way she said you'd fallen from heaven.
Had you tired of the Alone never being home?
Did you want the dead for your own?
I circled back. How to approach a hurt vulture?
Your wings were neatly folded.
Your bald nun's head was up, as if you were through
with prayer to a higher power–or was it real,
that whiff you caught again of flattened 'possum?
For he was afterward an hungred.

When I fell out of love, I would remember this.

The cricket frog called, *Drinks, drinks!*
or so you claimed, and there they were,
by the lake you'd borrowed.

The helmets of turtles surfaced, then sank,
guarding snagged tackle and old tires,
Atlantis in Florida.

Looking for one last fish to conquer,
an osprey ruled all but a dark cloud
above him, a border skirmish

best ignored—so Trajan would have advised
the younger Pliny out in Bithynia,
who was always writing,

The customary vows for your preservation,
sir. You can condescend to my worries
without injuring your dignity.

Dear Roman, those spiderwebs in the woods,
spun from horizon to tiny horizon
up a scaffold of dry stalks,

were the money spider's—I looked them up:
the conqueror waits for something
to try to walk on the silk.

Only the dew survives. Old Pliny would have loved
the snake you found in the understory:
the smallest one I'd ever seen,

a red knitting needle that wriggled away
into the tree unraveled by decay.
He was the one who,

having helped others into the boat,
stayed just a little longer
to watch Vesuvius

tuck Pompeii to sleep under the ash.
He saw Herculaneum bundled into the mud,
and then was overcome.

I pray the gods be willing for these words
to be held perpetually and sealed.

THE LATIN DOCTORS OF ARCHER CITY, TEXAS

I

Oil from long before Christ was pumped
by a cross between a pterodactyl
and a dipping toy duck.

Prickly pear, and a cactus submerged
in the clay up to its halo of spines—
like every other leaf,

they'd been nibbled and found wanting.
Red mud had dried and crazed
in a shallow bed

around the shell of a crayfish so well-cleaned,
it could have entered heaven. But still
a hermit could bloom

in the desert—there was just enough moisture.
But only if you were yellow, whatever
the shape of your petals—

if you found God in that godforsaken place,
you found he had a great fondness
for the yellow composite.

II

Somewhere past nowhere in the middle of Texas,
the air smelled of beef being fried,
no matter the hour.

Where a man's wealth had been measured
in barrels of crude or head of cattle,
now there was nothing.

In the old grocery store turned bookshop,
in the Medicine section,
stood a small, slim volume:

The Latin Doctors. O Ambrose, Augustine,
and Jerome, you seemed so at home
next to *Nervous Disorders.*

We repaired to the Lonesome Dove Inn,
once a tiny hospital.
Across the hall

from the white tiles of the old operating room,
in the Terms of Endearment Suite,
my love fell upon me,

as if in relief. Later, we drove past
the last house, a few doors down,
and the convenience store,

to the Great Plains. In a book of endless hours,
acres of palimpsest had been scraped clean
of mesquite, which grew right back.

In a dark corner of the museum,
        in the natural history
of the dark, I came to closed doors.
        They gave at my touch,
and I went in, but not before I read
        a warning to keep them shut,
and the next as well, lest butterflies escape.
        And then I was no longer
in New York in winter but in Florida—

        not just that balmy state
of mind but in my front yard, all overgrown.
        O heat! O humility!
I knew you well. In air made of water,
        I would sit on the porch
with the anoles, with whom I shared
        a cold-bloodedness,
as we waited to be moved to move.
        Sleepy Orange,

Gulf Fritillary, Queen and Gray Cracker—
        so those were your names,
my commoners. In the butterfly house
        you ignored me, too,
flower after flower. I was nothing to you,
        which was as it should be.
I meant so little in your scheme of things
        that I was brushed
on the cheek by a big Blue Morpho.

O iridescent wing,
as if of an angel by Van Eyck!
            One looking for blue,
any blue—even my sweater would do.
            No, one on the way
to someone else, whose hands would be spread
            as if to catch something
or let go, some woman willing to mother
            anyone sent her way.

To walk the unconscious, you must pass
    alligators lying on the verge
        of Florida. Basking
    like tread torn from a tire,
        black-rubbery,

not yet warmed up enough to move—
    what do you observe,
        dead Dr. Freud?
    Mud as black as your couch.
        Vultures roost

on the observation tower, as if it were time
    for another of the Divine Hours,
        all fifty minutes' worth.
    Their bald, red, sexual heads
        do not embarrass them.

Their dress nunlike, long and dark,
    they're waiting for death—
        not theirs—
    or a hot air current,
        whichever comes first.

Something slithers into the lake on your left.
    Something even larger bellows
        from the underbrush,
    warning you off—of what?
        The smell of rot

is just old alligator nests, on which you walk.
A female, hearing faint cries,
dug up her clutch—
like Ping-Pong balls gone soft.
Moons torn open—

look! She'll bear mothering a year or so,
teaching her squirming young
that you take
whatever moves away.
Waiting for prey,

birdwatchers alone hold as still
as the working reptile.
Good Doctor,
what do you wish the patient?
Ordinary unhappiness,

a lake drying up until the fish so concentrate
that the big wading birds,
busily feeding,
are undisturbed by the fact
you're only human.

"We have to get married," I said,
which stopped you cold in the aisle

of the antique store. What was the rush?
We'd been together twenty-five years.

I stood in front of an alligator
bride and groom as if I were priest,

justice of the peace, ship captain—
they weren't particular, who'd been waiting forever,

her lace yellowed, his black silk frayed.
They were too big, too leathery

to top a wedding cake, but I wanted them still—
two baby alligators who'd been stood up

on their hind legs, balanced by their tails,
stuffed, tanned, and dressed their best.

"We have to get married," I said.
What was I asking for? You'd given me a ring—

dredged from the Thames, still scratched
with the words *Be Tru in Hart*, too frail to wear.

Four glass eyes regarded us. Love,
give me your ungloved claw to hold.

in the museum of emptiness,
    I was just a tourist.
    The pages are blank,
no two alike—here is the catalogue.

Of a basin missing from its shelf,
    only the legend is left,
    how bear fought wolf
for a few words blazoned on a shield:

This is what happens if you want too much.
    The paw-to-paw combat
    would have been hidden
by a ewer, long lost, except when you washed

your hands of whomever you'd last touched.
    In the Middle Ages,
    I found myself middle-aged,
whole families of footfalls dying away

until I was left alone before a case
    that once held empty vessels,
    now doubly empty.
O pitcher with a pelican-beak spout,

in your absence I pour out nothing
    but this little air,
    and for no one,
not even a guard—he's gone to the Renaissance

in the next room, where a giraffe has appeared
　　　　in the story of Joseph
　　　　in exile, as painted
on a panel, once part of a coffin-size coffer.

O missing pharmacy jar, two-handed,
　　　　trace of a decoction
　　　　of rue dried inside!
We know nothing of such bitterness.

BIRDS OF AMERICA

The female also sings.

−from a field guide

I. Far South

And then one morning they left.
    Birds of good sense,
they waited for rain. All day it fell
    in buckets, in sheets,

but all the sandhill cranes wanted
    was what came after:
wind from the south, out of the Gulf
    one morning, late winter.

I heard the gates of heaven creak open,
    gates I no longer believed.
Braying, the great birds circled higher.
    Only I stood still

on a Self-Serv island at the Shell station,
    out of the way
of my life, as if I'd left it at last,
    or you, at least.

A vulture, sure *it* owned the warm air
    on which it rose,
was swept into the swirl. Its only way out
    of heading north, too,

was to flap its wings. So lesser birds, not meant
    to soar, must do.
O the indignity! Like the professor I was,
    in its black feathers

it could lecture on love—love, the dead thing
    it smelled for lunch.
Life smelled of gasoline and tanning lotion
    in Florida, where,

out of a sky scrubbed clean of cloud
    came the great clatter
of those who mated for life. Stay together!
    No, stay together!

On the grounds of a villa on the river,
    we laid our lunch,
my parents and I. Did they love each other?
    They stood apart in the wind.

They shooed peacocks off the picnic tables.
    All aflutter,
the blue-eyed tail of a male snapped open
    to flatter a peahen,

who turned her back—but not, as I thought,
    from lack of interest.
Miles from anywhere, at Maryhill,
    the wind up the gorge

had nothing to do but come between us,
    having bent the trees.
Having bent everything but the mansion—
    Italianate,

made of concrete, this was the house
    Sam Hill built
for his wife back East, who didn't want it.
    Fifty years late,

we'd come to see the latest fashions
    for 1947—
the year my mother, in borrowed dress,
    married my father.

They passed each other food as if nothing—
        or something—had passed
between them, though they didn't touch.
        Was this happiness?

The bluebirds of Bicker—no, *Bickle*ton—
        were our next stop:
deeper blues, and that soft cry, the *few*,
        the happy *few, few, few.*

V

"What kind of film are you using?"
"Sixteen-millimeter color," said Laurence.
The Marine thought for a moment. "If you're shooting
color, you really ought to go down to Khe Sanh, because of the
beautiful greens and browns," he said. "You know, they have
six different shades of green down there."

–Michael Arlen

In the middle of my life, I found myself
in a swamp, having lost my way.
It's hard to say what way that was.

Full of leaf-fall, water as tannic as tea—
the skin of anything that drowned in there
would be turned to leather.

How I got there I can't say. I was asleep,
looking for a place to park. I was still in town—
no, just south, the car sinking

into the ground, sun coming up
over the quaggy water. Over a log with eyes,
which slowly opened: an alligator

nosing its way through the waterweed.
Booming like a cannon, it called for a mate,
the air atremble with outlandish longing.

Mud was sucking at my mock-crocodile shoe
when someone appeared, faint from long silence.
In that everglade, I called out, *Are you dead or alive?*

ON THE OREGON TRAIL

Here dons, grandees, but chiefly dames abound,
Skill'd in the ogle of a roguish eye,
Yet ever well inclined to heal the wound;
None through their cold disdain are doom'd to die,
As moon-struck bards complain, by Love's sad archery.

—Lord Byron

After literature came lunch,
then archery, a sport deemed suitable
for the young ladies who boarded at a small college
on the Oregon Trail. We could have been

all corsets and crinolines instead of miniskirts.
"Let the bow arm hang down,"
the professor of physical education said,
"as though holding a small suitcase."

We took position. We'd seen the wagon ruts,
the grassy remains of the mission
where the local tribes had been given
proper clothes, new names, and a fever.

In the dollhouse of a diorama,
a stiff figure sat on a chair brought over the pass
along with a wife—our founder, Dr. Whitman.
He counted up his converts, his back to a tomahawk.

His wife was next, and then twelve others.
At Waiilatpu, Place of the Rye Grass,
wild grain bowed its seed-heavy heads
to what the white man calls Indian summer.

Backs straight, we sat in the dorm-mother's room,
ankles crossed, and listened to the voice of God:
Walter Cronkite read the evening news.
In Walla Walla our archery

was laughed at by the boys in ROTC.
Weekly they drilled, down at the far end
of the green, so as not to be sent
to some small war much farther off.

On television the men still alive and running
for president looked engraved, waving away,
balloons drifting down as prettily as bombs.

Another Kennedy was dead, but that was in June.
Where was the soap opera I always watched?
Where its lovers, last seen fleeing from the story

in a car stolen like a kiss? Where the crash
from which Venus would rise, sporting a fake
black eye? Her Mars had the shifty eyes of McNamara.

I was just nineteen. What did I know
about the love of lies, the lies of love?
Alone, I rode the bus to the big green city.

I stumped among the flowers, big as plates,
that lined the walks. Dahlias.
I'd never seen the like. They nodded curly heads;

I held out promises of water—but they had rain.
O Seattle, the town that Boeing built!
Plane after plane, it loved that little war,

the one that couldn't be won from the air.

THE MALE MODEL

Look back in Ingres
—art school graffito, 1968

And, said the professor of drawing,
whatever part of the model we failed to draw
he'd take us down to the wood shop and cut off.

The ex-nun blushed. The soldier's wife blanched.
The college boys—what were their draft numbers?
The young man with an empty sleeve

went on drawing the way we all did,
charcoal in the hand that did the rubbing out,
which surely followed. Where was the skeleton

who'd held a pose forever all last week?
I missed its bones of yellowed plastic.
Today's model, male, had muscles that braided

like water under a skin of the darkest marble—
so this was why Michelangelo,
to make a woman, had carved another David

and given him breasts. He called her Night.
Let *her* pose for us, she who can barely sleep
without slipping off the tomb she guards

in that far corner of art history forever Florence.
A minor Medici neither poet nor murderer,
famous for nothing, the dead man looks

the other way, with someone else's head.

An inch of snow,
and Seattle skidded to a halt.
Silence fell, a foot or more,
on Capitol Hill, on Beacon and Queen Anne.

Worthless, my degree in art.
What would Madame Nhu, late of Saigon, do,
that deposed dictator's wife
who said you could sleep on the run,

but only in a *couture* coat?
Dante, in exile, you sat in the Latin Quarter,
out in the open on straw,
to hear Aquinas convert Aristotle.

Did nothing act
but with an eye to evil? Twenty years from now
I'd stand at the corner
of the Rue Dante, having lost my faith;

now I turned classmate
to veterans, ex-convicts, single mothers,
all to be rehabilitated,
apprentices to the printer's trade.

Paper drifted like snow,
blank reams misfed through the press.
Walking home on ice,
I took a further fall from grace.

What silence, shattered
by the simple sound of a shovel–O Valéry!
In that cold circle
what good was your French, the language

of love and Dien Bien Phu?

Leaves came and went, and still men warred,
    even in Paris.
There they argued the shape of the table

    at which to talk peace,
there in that city where Ho Chi Minh
    had been young once,

hungry and hunted. Veteran of another war,
    all my father wanted
was no squabbles at the supper table.

    What shape should it take
to insure that we were out of range
    of one another?

Supper would be cold, milk spilled,
    one of us seven
sent from the room before it was over.

    After it was over,
down in the basement, my father sat
    enthroned on a La-Z-Boy

on its last legs, the remote control of the TV
    at his right hand.
He taught himself to flake an arrowhead.

     Pressure from above
forced one fracture after another
    from the underside

of the obsidian. He bandaged a finger.
    We'd bomb them
back to the Stone Age, the Southern senator said.

I. The Art of Painting

after Vermeer

She looked too young to be History,
    the woman in blue
      whose eyes were closed.
Mouth gone slack, she held a trumpet

as if for someone else, and a hide-bound book,
    both about to slip.
      In front of a map
out of date even in 1666, she stood still.

Past folds and tears painted as lovingly
    as rivers lay Holland,
      not yet torn in two,
Catholic from Calvinist. New Amsterdam

traded for Surinam—she turned her back
    on the golden age.
      Turned from the window—
she *must* be History: she knew not to look,

or she might see the salt mine where the Führer,
    that failed art student,
      would keep the painting safe.
Or might meet the gaze of the dandy in black velvet

hogging the foreground, starting her portrait
    with that silly crown
      of laurel leaves, too blue.
A Turkish curtain snagged on an empty chair—

sit down. He wants us to watch
            over his shoulder.
            Over their heads,
the Ocean of Germany swims with shoes—

no, wooden ships. From the East Indies,
            two teardrop pearls
            for her middle-class ears.
In her name, what price hasn't been paid?

The famous poet read out loud
    a famous poem
      about a fish, not his.
On and on it went, letting out line

just the way my father had advised,
    the art of fishing
      lost on me. A worm
threaded on a hook: he'd shown me how

it had to wriggle, half on, half off.
    I had to hold still–
      and for what?
In that backwater, bullhead were biting.

The fish I caught almost accidentally,
    then couldn't throw back
      or whack on a rock,
swam in a bucket the long way home.

It chased itself along the perimeter,
    whiskers bristling.
      Did we bury it
in the garden, or eat fish for supper?

I don't remember. In the late imperial age,
    in poetry class,
      we wrote no epics
of a little war. We wrote of love or its lack.

On the day of the dead, the Roman was right,
    a poet should sacrifice
      to a goddess who kept mute,
one who was a fish with her mouth sewn shut.

The man was dead but the soldiers weren't through.
Nor was the artist,
who prepared the plate
for the acid bath, stopping out the sky

and then the great coat of the soldier
who held the dead man
by one bent leg.
But nothing blinded like the paper

Goya left blank to make the sword shine,
there where the blade
began to castrate.
But for the trunk of a tree, sawn off,

and a single leafy shoot, waiting to be shot,
the landscape lay empty,
as if nothing dared stand
but memory, longing to be laid to rest.

Behind each new disaster of war
he put the place
he'd been born,
where a dusty road lay down outside the hut

and refused to go on. He went on.
He fought the bulls
when he was hungry.
First Painter to the King, he painted

the royal family bejeweled
    as if with spittle.
    He painted a woman
with her clothes on and without,

the *maja* naked all the Inquisitors cared about.
    What didn't kill him
    made him deaf,
the better not to hear. And the eyes?

One has two too many, said the pretty soldier
    Rilke sent riding to battle
    on a velvet saddle,
but that was an earlier war—or was it later?

There was no hill any more, hardly a tree.
    Nothing dared stand,
    not even the light.
It lay collapsed on the muddy boots.

It crawled up to the knees. It peered
    into the hands,
    the faces gone dark.
I looked away. I looked back.

Debora Greger is the author of six previous books of poetry. She has won, among other honors, the Grolier Prize, the Discovery–*The Nation* prize, the Lavan Younger Poets Award from the Academy of American Poets, an Award in Literature from the American Academy and Institute of Arts and Letters, and the Brandeis University Award for Poetry. She teaches at the University of Florida and lives in Gainesville, Florida, and in Cambridge, England.

TED BERRIGAN
Selected Poems
The Sonnets

PHILIP BOOTH
Lifelines

JIM CARROLL
Fear of Dreaming
Void of Course

BARBARA CULLY
Desire Reclining

CARL DENNIS
*New and Selected Poems
1974–2004*
Practical Gods

DIANE DI PRIMA
Loba

STUART DISCHELL
Dig Safe

STEPHEN DOBYNS
*Pallbearers Envying the
One Who Rides*
The Porcupine's Kisses

ROGER FANNING
Homesick

AMY GERSTLER
Crown of Weeds
Ghost Girl
Medicine
Nerve Storm

DEBORA GREGER
*Desert Fathers, Uranium
Daughters*
God
Western Art

ROBERT HUNTER
Sentinel

BARBARA JORDAN
Trace Elements

MARY KARR
Viper Rum

JACK KEROUAC
Book of Blues
Book of Haikus

JOANNE KYGER
As Ever

ANN LAUTERBACH
If in Time
On a Stair

PHYLLIS LEVIN
Mercury

WILLIAM LOGAN
Macbeth in Venice
Night Battle
Vain Empires

DEREK MAHON
Selected Poems

MICHAEL McCLURE
*Huge Dreams: San
Francisco and Beat
Poems*

CAROL MUSKE
An Octave Above Thunder

ALICE NOTLEY
The Descent of Alette
Disobedience
Mysteries of Small Houses

LAWRENCE RAAB
The Probable World
Visible Signs

PATTIANN ROGERS
Generations

STEPHANIE
STRICKLAND
V

ANNE WALDMAN
Kill or Cure
Marriage: A Sentence
*Structure of the World
Compared to a Bubble*

JAMES WELCH
Riding the Earthboy 40

PHILIP WHALEN
Overtime: Selected Poems

ROBERT WRIGLEY
Lives of the Animals
Reign of Snakes

JOHN YAU
Borrowed Love Poems